Artigiana Studi

CW01315578

REFURBISH YOUR FURNITURE

DIY AT HOME

My Projects

PROJECT _____

NAME _____

TOOLS NEEDED _____
_____

MATERIALS _____
_____
_____
_____

COLORS USED _____

My Projects

PROJECT

NAME _____

TOOLS NEEDED _____

_____

MATERIALS _____

_____

_____

_____

COLORS USED _____

My Projects

Look back at the chapter called "Tools needed" and prepare your shopping list here.

SHOPPING LIST

_____

_____

_____

_____

_____

_____

_____

_____

Before

After

After

Before

Thank you!

Final assembly

You've finished all the painting, varnishing, maybe even given it an antique patina, now it's time to carefully assemble all the pieces: doors, hinges, hardware, knobs, or handles.
All that's left is to enjoy the resulting new product and find a suitable place in your home to show it off.

You'll be surprised to see at the end how good the furniture looks that at first you thought you wouldn't keep.

Today's design specialists are very much in favor of combining old and new, classic, and modern, and a desk, a wardrobe, a chair painted in the right color will provide the color balance you need.

Congratulations!

Tip: you are ready for your first project!

... more finishing

A very interesting look is given by the metallic patina discreetly applied, they enhance the furniture.

The most beautiful effects are achieved with bronze patinas. Used with care, gold also gives an interesting, precious look. Copper pattina is also an option. But keep in mind that less is more, so use patinas carefully.

Tip: patina can also be made by mixing transparent wax with colouring powder, gold or antique bronze

Final finishing

To accentuate the aged look, you can use ageing patinas. These are generally dark colors (walnut, dark walnut), but also green patinas (like mold or bluish-grey ones, like weathered wood that give an authentic look. In the case of furniture that has been painted and then sanded on the edges, the patina is applied all over. Patinas that are sanded with abrasive sponges after application or patinas that are applied by wiping can be used.

A very interesting look can be achieved by structuring the wood, bringing out the pattern of late wood and early wood. Late wood, being harder, remains in relief and early wood, being softer, is removed superficially. So, when you run your hand perpendicularly over the wood you will feel its raised pattern. You can achieve the effect by using round wire brushes fitted to a drill.
The furniture must be made of solid wood.

Tip: the design of the furniture requires the right type of antiquing

Final finishing

The easiest way to make a piece of furniture look old is to paint it a different color, then sand the edges to the original color or even wood. The process is called distressing or edge-burning. It's simple to do, and if the color is applied with a brush, the old effect is even more pronounced. Because it is possible to get to the wood when sanding the edges, it is best to apply a clear varnish on top. The varnish doesn't have to be very glossy because it's hard to believe that old furniture shines. For finishes like this, use low-gloss varnishes with a natural effect. So it is better to choose a matt finish varnish or a satin one. Before applying the varnish, check the compatibility of the coats, but usually they are compatible especially if both are water-based.

If you want an even more antique or rustic look, you can also sand directly on the surface of the furniture. But make sure that nothing looks unnatural. Tip: try to imagine where the furniture might normally be knocked and sand there. Always have the big picture in front of you, the furniture as a whole, don't think of each door or drawer individually. They may look great separately, but together the whole thing becomes overdone, out of touch with reality, so it won't not look like scratched furniture.

Tip: the design of the furniture requires the right type of antiquing

... more painting

Water-based varnishes were designed to last. They can be used both indoors and outdoors because they contain UV protection, so outdoor pieces won't fade over time. Being water-based, the varnish does not yellow. It is recommended on any piece of furniture that comes into direct contact with water or anywhere we have a high traffic surface, and it is important that it is hard-wearing and durable. It is available in three versions: matt, satin, and gloss, depends on what you prefer for the final look.

If the wooden pieces you are refurbishing will be placed in the yard, so in an outdoor environment, it is advisable to use an oil-based paint, so that the color is preserved, and the object is protected in the rain. Outdoor varnish with UV protection is another option.

Why water-based paints or vanishes?
- they dry much more easily
- they don't give off odors or toxins

Tip: don't worry if the first coat of paint doesn't look great, the second coat will solve it

... more painting

Being water-based, paints must be sealed. This is not a negligible phase; it is as important as painting. Sealing is done to make the surface wear-resistant, waterproof, and easy to clean. You can use two products for sealing: wax or water-based varnish. Wax is found in liquid, paste or solid form. Application is easy, you can use a brush if it's in liquid form or a soft cloth if it's solid or paste form. Wax gives a natural, matt, and velvety look to furniture. There are several types here too, but the most important one is the base wax, which is colorless or transparent and has the function of protecting the painted surface. Colored waxes are used depending on the design: Dark Wax for a vintage look, Black Wax for industrial style and White Wax for a shabby chic look. Please note: used without the base wax, colored waxes change the color of the painted surface completely. Wax is applied with a special wax brush, or a lint-free cloth. After application the excess must be wiped off. Clean the waxed surface with a damp cloth. It behaves like new furniture: it is not scratch-resistant, nor resistant to high temperatures, so do not put hot mugs on it, nor it is resistant to abundant water. It will be waterproof, but the water must be wiped off immediately, otherwise it can leave marks. In case of damage, the waxed surface can be easily corrected, repainted, and waxed locally. After a few years, repeated waxing is recommended. Wax dries in 24 hours, but has a curing period of 14/21 days, which also depends on temperature and air humidity. During this time the furniture can be used, but more carefully. It is not recommended for outdoor use.

Tip: if you have chosen wax finish, try to avoid water on furniture, it may leave marks on it

Painting process

Once your furniture is ready, clean, and dry, you can start painting. If you want to paint several pieces of furniture the same color, make sure you have the right amount of paint, specially if you have combined colors together. Carefully read the manufacturer's instructions on paint consumption per surface size.

You can use a paint specially designed for wood surfaces and apply it in two or three coats, depending on the degree of coverage. Whichever paint you choose to use it is important to respect the drying times recommended by the manufacturer, even if the surface may appear dry to the touch, do not rush the paint by applying the next coat. You can use a water-based paint for interior fixtures,intended for wood.

There are several types of water-based paints, plain, chalky, and non-chalk, and recently water-based enamels have appeared. If you use enamels you can choose from the start the finish, as with varnishes, to be matt, satin, or glossy and they do not require further varnishing. They are preferable for furniture items such as shelves and dressers, as they shorten the painting process and get you to the finish faster. However, if it's a table or chairs, it would be better to use a water-based paint sealed with two-coat varnish or wax, as you'll have longer-lasting protection and resistance to mechanical knocks, as these are frequently used fixtures.

Once you have chosen the right tool for your project, you can apply the coats of paint. Respect the drying time between coats indicated by the manufacturer, this time can vary depending on the temperature and humidity of the air, but of course also on the quality of the surface.

Tip: always look back to avoid drops, and try to find a selfleveling paint, it will help you to get a smoot surface

... more priming tips

Two coats of primer are required and only then start the painting process.

You should treat the primer just like another coat of paint, so you can apply it with brush, paintbrush or spray gun.

Tip: sand lightly, by hand, with a low-grit sandpaper, 320 or 400 between primer coats, so you have removed any possible impurities

Using a primer

At some older pieces of furniture there is a risk of tannins. Tannins in wood can be troublesome, both because of their acidic nature and because they are soluble in water, and some of them even in organic solvents.
All trees contain tannin, both in the root and the trunk. The color of the tannin ranges from reddish yellow to brown. The lighter the color of the wood, the less tannin it contains. High tannin content is found in oak, chestnut, acacia, walnut, mahogany, and most exotic species with a more pronounced color. If a tannin wood splinter is left out in the rain, it will stain and remain so after drying. It is possible to remove the stained surface by sanding, but on first contact with water the phenomenon will recur.

By applying water-based paints or varnishes, we allow the tannins to dissolve and migrate to the surface of the wood. The presence of tannins is not signaled by a specific appearance, so it is hard to know whether the wood will stain or not.

This is where the importance of the primer comes in again, to have the power to cover the tannins, to avoid their penetration through the paint and result in a finished product with yellowish-brown stains.

Tip: use a high coverage primer

Using a primer

I've sanded, then I've covered all the scratches with putty, I've sanded again now comes the primer.

Why should we use primer?

The primer is specially formulated to treat wood and provide a base for the paint coat. It should therefore be applied directly to the wood after it has been prepared. To achieve adhesion to the substrate, the primer penetrates as deeply as possible, anchoring itself as well as possible to the wood, thus making an easy transition to the paint. In addition, it gives the paint better resistance to possible mechanical knocks and makes the painting process easier.

Another important aspect is consumption. A properly primed surface will not absorb as much paint, which lowers our costs, as primer is much cheaper than paint.

Tip: use a high coverage primer

Putty

Any scratches or deep dents are repaired with wood putty and a putty knife, also named as chuck or stripper. Make sure it's a special wood putty, looks like a white paste and with the help of the tool will perfectly fill in every scratch.

Don't panic if there are deeper holes that need to be covered, in this situation you may need to fill with putty twice. Just wait for the first coat of putty to dry.

After the putty has dried, sand again until the entire surface is even and smooth to the touch. Use a small grit sandpaper, like 220.

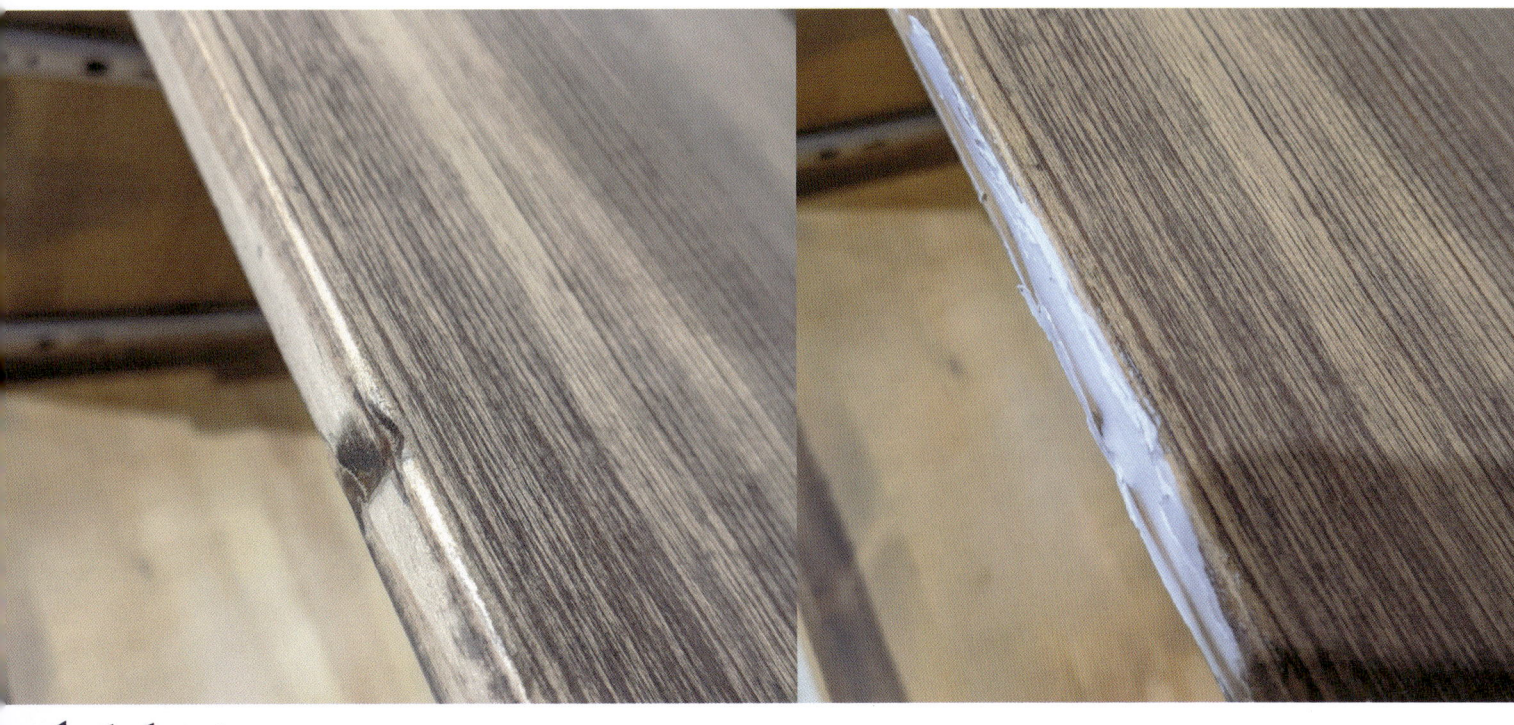

Tip: Try to find a light putty, it will fill in the smallest scratches

...more sanding tips

If the furniture you want to refurbish is veneer, don't even try to sand it by hand because you won't succeed. For this you will definitely need an orbital sander. By hand, you won't be able to get an even finish.

Tip: these scratches cannot be removed by hand sanding

Sanding phase

After degreasing the furniture, the extremely important sanding stage follows. It is recommended to sand the wood with sandpaper for wood.

This is different from metal sandpaper, so you should be careful when buying it. You can use a hand sanding block, which has direct Velcro hooks and will make it easier to press the area you want to sand. But, be careful to buy sandpaper that can be attached to velcro hooks.

Sandpaper grits are expressed in figures, so if you need to sand a thicker layer, choose a higher grit of 40, 80 or 120. If you need the sanding to be as fine as possible, choose a smaller grit of 220, 320, 400.

If the furniture does not show large scratches you can sand directly with 220 grit.

Sand the furniture by hand, it just takes a little bit longer. If your budget allows, you may want to use an orbital sander, as this will take less time and the sanding will be even. It is also at this stage that you will decide whether to use a method of stripping the old paint using a paint stripper or removing the paint using a hot air gun. If you are able to remove the old paint by sanding, there is no need to strip it.

The sanding stage is completed by wiping off the dust, either by vacuuming or with a soft, dry cloth.

Tip: If the furniture is not badly damaged on the surface, you can easily sand by hand. The orbital sander helps you move faster.

Surface preparation

The first thing you must do is to clean the piece of furniture so that it is completely clean, dry, without deposits or marks on the surface such as wax, varnish, dirt, dust, which then prevent the application of paint.

You can use a damp cloth and a little detergent if the surface is dirtier. You can also use denaturated alcohol it is extremely versatile and a powerful furniture degreaser.

Pay close attention to surfaces that are more exposed than others such as countertops, shelves, handles on chairs, corners that are wiped less often, etc.

For example for cleaning the legs of a table that has embossed decorative elements, you could use an old toothbrush to clean off all the old dust and grease deposits.

Remove all hardware such as handles, knobs, hinges, decorative metal elements that you do not want to paint by mistake.

Tip: Remove the handles before starting

Types of wood

Always when starting any refurbishment project, the first step is a careful analysis of the product. We look at the wood it is made of, whether it has been painted before, if it shows signs of knocks or damage, if it needs any kind of repair to drawers, handles, hardware, etc.

Furniture that needs refurbishing or we simply want to change its color can be made of different types of wood that need to be treated differently.

Furniture made of pallet or mdf
- It is the newest type of wood found today
- Requires light sanding as it has quite shiny surfaces
- A primer with high adhesion to various surfaces is recommended

Natural wood furniture
- If it has never been painted before, it needs a clear primer
- Sand only if necessary
- Apply primer and then paint

Furniture with old paint
- First the old paint should be removed, either by sanding or using a paint stripper or hot air blower (this is not quite an easy process)
- Sand and grout the imperfections, then sand the grout again.
- Only after these stepts can come the primer and then paint

Furniture made with varnished, painted, or veneered wood
- Remove old varnish or paint layers by sanding or stripping
- Putty if is necessary
- Proceed to priming, then painting

Tip: with the right approach, any type of wood can be painted

Work steps

When we want to refurbish a piece of furniture, there are always important steps to follow, and we should not change their order or skip some steps because it seems too long. It's good to follow the steps in order to have the desired result in the end.
The first step is a careful analysis of the piece of furniture: we observe what it was painted with before, if it needs repairing, if it has dents, we remove old hardware (hinges, knobs, handles), we make a list of items that need replacing, on a case-by-case basis. These stages are:

- Surface preparation for painting
- Sanding, putty and primer
- The actual painting
- Final assembly

Tip: If the furniture is too damaged, consider whether it is worth the cost of replacing parts

Painting method

- We use trafalto when we want to get a very uniform surface. It can be made of sponge or velvet, depending on the paint used and our skill, we choose the one that suits us best.
- We use the spray gun or sprayer when we want a perfect surface, like new, factory-new, but we must keep in mind that spraying gives off paint fumes and for this reason we must have a special room for this operation, otherwise everything around will have paint stains.

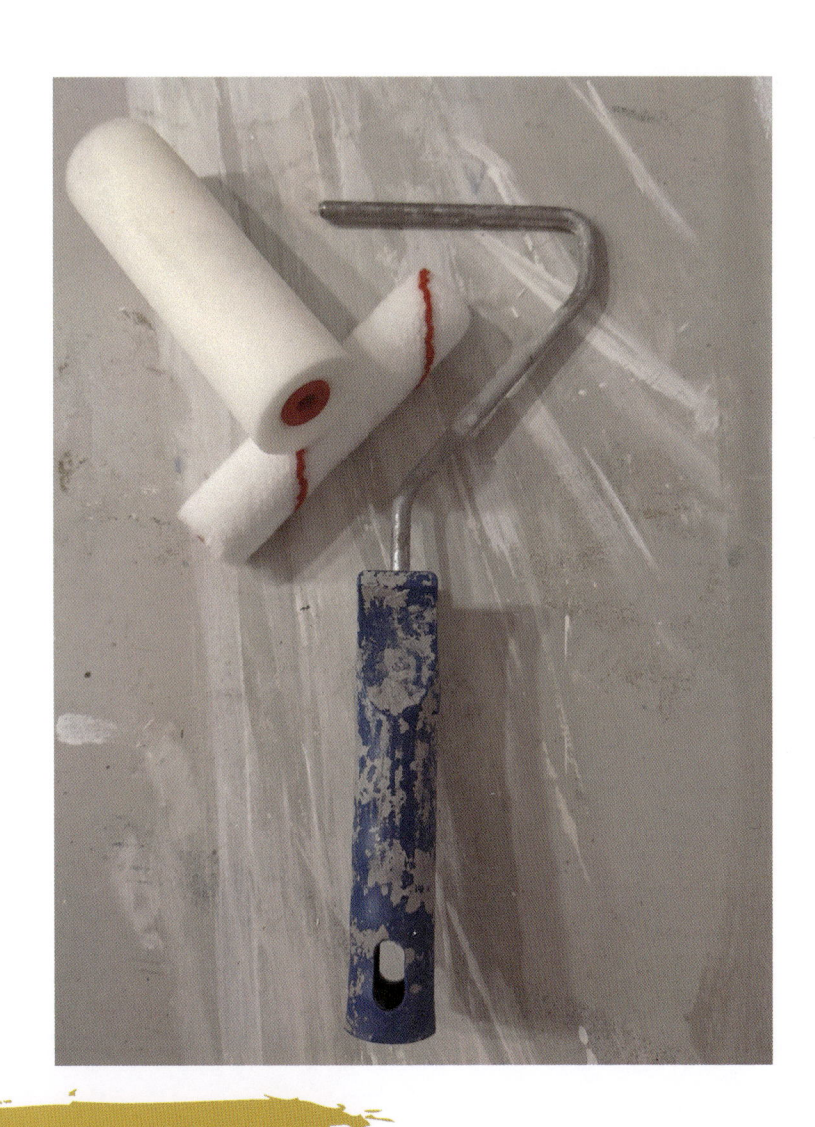

Tip: Trafalto is also a very easy tool to use for beginners

Painting method

Brushes, rollers, or paint gun - how do we choose? We make our choice according to the final look we want and the paints we use. Tools help us create all kinds of surfaces with them, from vintage, textured, antiqued, to modern and smooth.

- Round or oval brushes are used to achieve the vintage, rustic look. These brushes are very dense, made of natural pig hair, therefore they leave brush marks, with them you can achieve textures, which give a unique character to the furniture.
- Flat brushes are used when we want a smooth, modern look. These brushes are made of artificial bristles, their tips are either tapered or cut straight to work very smoothly. If it's of good quality, no brush marks will remain. They come in various sizes, the large one is recommended for large surfaces, doors, countertops, shelves, and the small ones for edges, corners, skirting boards.

Tip: To get you started I recommend you choose the brush.

chuck

sanding paper

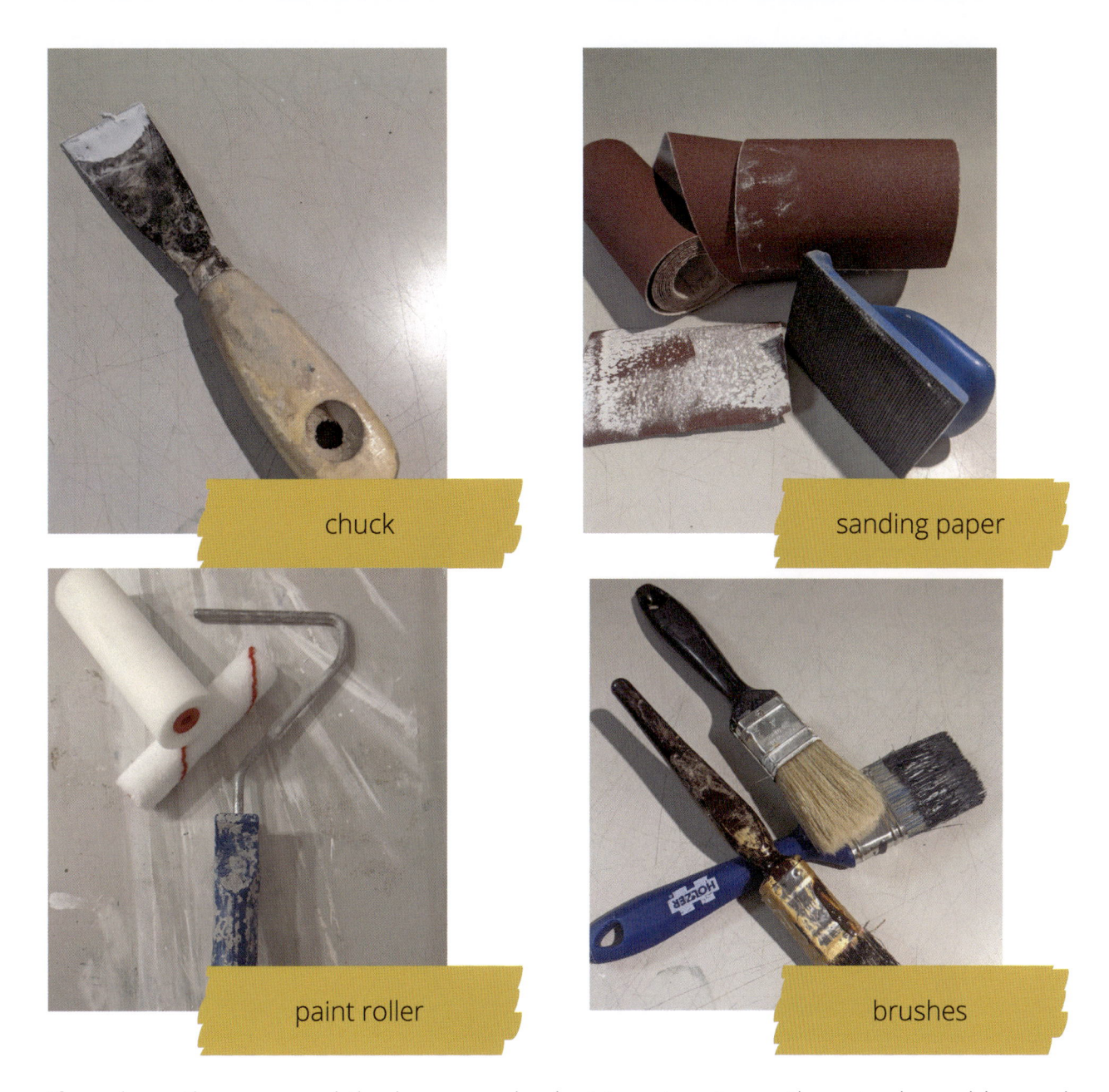

paint roller

brushes

If you have them around the house, or budget is not an issue, these tools could speed up some of the work:

- orbital sander with sandpaper with high, medium, and low grain, so that the material is fine and smooth
- drill

For more complex refurbishments that involve reshaping, replacing legs or countertops, consider the following tools:

- wood planer
- drill
- normal hammer and rubber hammer screws and nails
- saw

Tools needed

Whether you want to refurbish a bulky piece of furniture, a chair, or a coffee table, there are certain steps and materials you should consider having on hand.

- abrasive sponge / sanding paper for sanding
- brushes, paintbrushes or trafalto
- chuck - special knife used to fill the small holes with putty
- measuring tool - roulette, ruler, etc.
- orbital sander
- wood putty - used for repairing and filling any imperfections
- primer - to apply before paint for better paint adhesion
- paint
- varnish
- safety equipment - gloves, mask
- paint gun - depending on the painting method chosen

*** if you decide to use a paint gun, you should consider that it needs a little more investment. The paint gun also needs a proper compressor, a mechanical device that increases the pressure, with several specifications depending on painting method. Another important aspect is the room for painting, you have to consider a dedicated space for using a paint gun, because of the vapours.

Safety measures

No matter how hard you try to avoid dust, when you want to refurbish and paint a piece of furniture, you won't succeed. It's going to be dusty, and if you don't have the ability to do this process outside, then start by choosing a room to work in. Painting furniture is an easy activity you can do in your spare time. However, it is important to follow a few protective measures:

- Air out room you are painting, open windows, doors and don't let anyone stay in that room overnight, least of all elderly people, children, pets.

- Use a fan if the room cannot be properly ventilated naturally.

- During the sanding stage wear a dust mask, goggles, and textile work gloves.

- When painting, use rubber gloves and a mask with replaceable filters to protect your lungs.

- Clean and cover the floor of the room where you are painting the piece of furniture with a cloth material, not plastic, because you can slip.

- Do not paint or store paint near any heat source, or any type of flames.

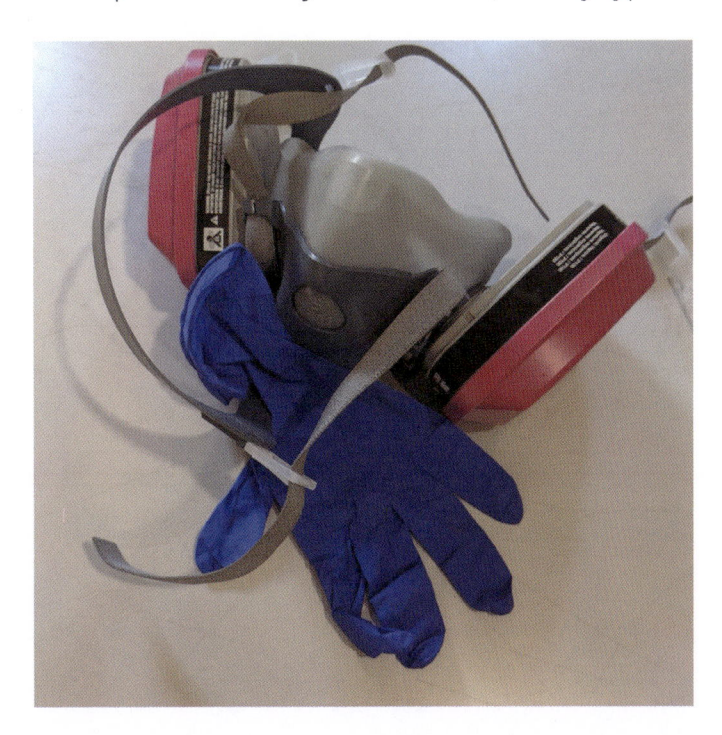

Short introduction

Refurbishing furniture is simple and fun - that's what you can hear wherever you start reading on the subject.

Yes, it can be fun and simple if you know what it's about, otherwise it can just be a source of nerves and a waste of time. This book is just what you need, it comes to your aid by dissolving your doubts, giving you an easy, understandable guide. You don't need big budgets or sophisticated and expensive tools, just a little skill and a lot of patience.

Before starting any refurbishment process, the most important thing is to consider whether the product is worth refurbishing. If the product has a lot of defects, is missing basic elements, is rotten or needs a lot of processing, may not be worth refurbishing because it is already in an advanced process of degradation. Do not confuse the term refurbishment with restoration. Basically, the restoration process brings the same product back to life in the same shape and detail as it was originally designed, replacing for example legs that have rotted, handles that have broken and keeping the same color tones. Reconditioning refers to the creation of a new product, with a different look, color, or shape according to preference.

I will share with you all that I have learned over the years broken down into stages of work. The book is aimed at beginners and brings together all the information I wish I had been able to read myself when painting furniture was just a hobby for me. In the meantime, it has become one of my core activities.

But what you need to know from the start: every project is unique!

There is no one-size-fits-all method. Either the surface differs, or the tools, or even the temperature at which we work. All circumstances need to be taken into account when you start working. You will never find exactly the same situations with different pieces of furniture, but I can say with confidence that if you read carefully and follow the steps described in the book, you will succeed in creating something special. With each completed project, you will in turn accumulate a wealth of information that will help you in the future.

Table of contents

Short introduction 1
Safety measures 2
Tools needed 3
Painting method 5
Work steps 7
Types of wood 8
Surface preparation 9
Sanding phase 10
Putty 12
Using a primer 13
Painting process 16
Final finishing 19
Final assembly 22

Printed in Great Britain
by Amazon